Photography   POCKET EDITION

PHOTOGRAPHY BASICS AND TECHNIQUE

The ISBN is: 9781718058002

ZAC DELANE, LARRY HAMMER

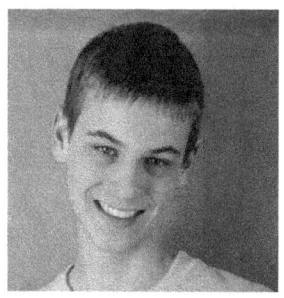

ABOUT ZAC DELANE

Zac DeLane is the main author of The Digital Way series. He is currently a High Schooler and has a deep passion for education, photography, videography and design. He holds Adobe Certifications in Visual Arts, Web Technologies and Graphic Design. As well, he has won awards from the UIL of Texas for his work on videos and is a certified Apple Teacher. He resides in Austin, Texas with his family.

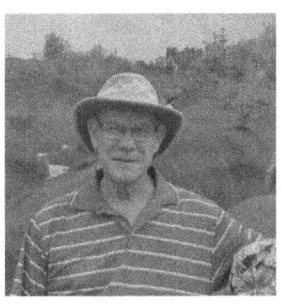

ABOUT LARRY HAMMER

Larry Hammer is Zac's Grandpa who resides in San Antonio, Texas. He is a retired engineer and Vietnam War Vet. He has developed a passion for photography, and participates in a photography forum, The Ugly Hedgehog. He is a contributer and fact checker for this book. He and his wife like to travel across America, taking photos along the way.

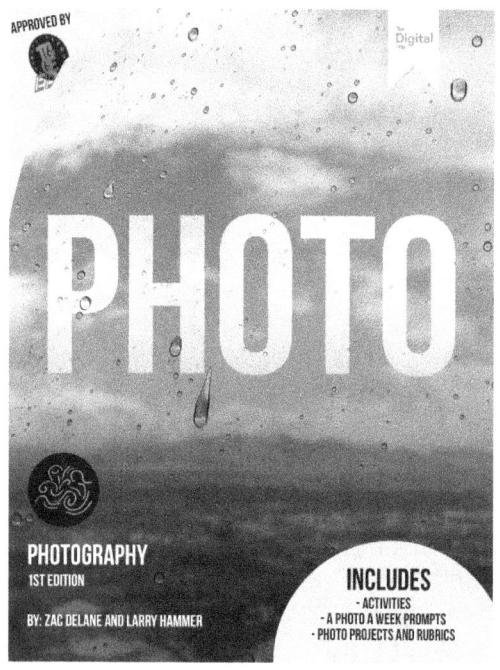

While this pocket edition is nifty and all, we recommend checking out our main book, which includes more activity files, more information and *A Photo a Week* prompts.

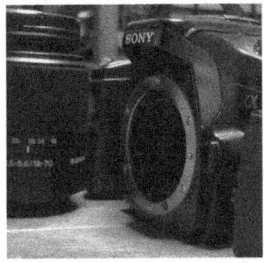

Section 1: Knowing the Body
Section 2: Lenses
Section 3: Additional Equipment

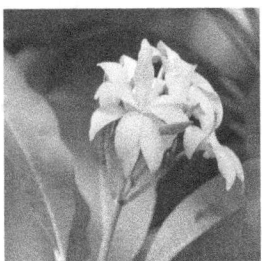

Section 1: Understanding Mood
Section 2: Using Lighting
Section 3: Positioning your Subject
Section 4: Preparing the Camera

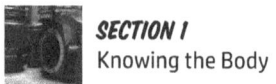

SECTION I
Knowing the Body

It may seem complex, but a DSLR camera is one of the most powerful and professional cameras you'll find out there. It also may seem confusing at first. In this section, I want to describe the body of the camera and clear the confusion of any terminology that may appear on a modern day DSLR camera.

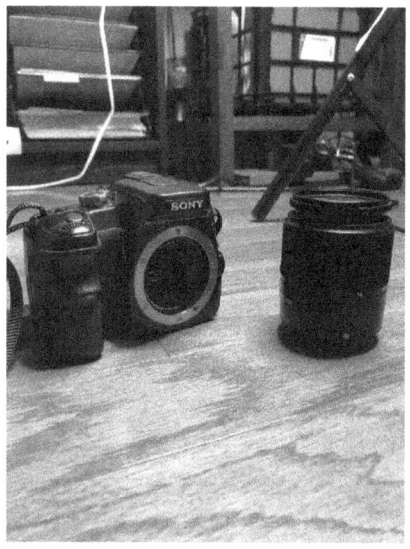

As you can see in this picture, this is known as the DSLR Camera. You'll see the **body** of the camera and the **lens** next to it. This is a major feature of the DSLR camera too. The ability to detach a lens from the frame and switch it to another frame allows for maximum customization and opportunity for photographers. Some retailers will only sell the Frame without a lens so that photographers can pick and choose what lens they want vs paying for the default ones that they may not want.

Most, if not all, cameras will have different preset modes for users to choose from. These modes makes it easier for photographers and commoners to easily customize the presets to the environment they're in. For instance, some cameras will include a Sport mode, increasing the shutter speed to capture high and fast moving objects. These presets make it easier for anyone to pick up a DSLR camera to use it.

Yet, as professional photographers will tell you, these presets won't cut it. In order to be successful, you'll need to break past the presets to customize to your specific scenario.

CAMERA TERMINOLOGY

As you get to customizing the settings of the camera to your needs, you may encounter some terms you may not know. I'll discuss and show some examples of these terms in action.

First theres **Exposure.** Exposure is the fundamental principle of photography. This determines how much light is allowed to inter the camera's body through the lens's aperture and expose an image on the sensor. Lighting, as we will discuss later, will make or break your photography. It sets the mood and tone of your photos. Having bad lighting will result in a poor photo.

Shutter Speed is the speed of the shutter opening and closing. A photo is created by the shutter (within the lens) opening and closing repetitively. By altering this speed, you can create different effects and photos.

Aperture refers to the opening through the diaphragm of the lens. This helps set the exposure. Generally, this is represented in the form of f/.

> *The lower the f/stop—the larger the opening in the lens—the less depth of field—the blurrier the background.*
>
> *The higher the f/stop—the smaller the opening in the lens—the greater the depth of field—the sharper the background.*

-via https://www.nikonusa.com

Just know that Aperture is one of the controls in the lens that you can change as needed to capture an image with good exposure. The only thing you can alter is the Aperture Priority on the camera.

I want to discuss how important Exposure is. While many cameras have automatic technology to adjust the lighting and exposure in a shot to prevent over exposure, you need to be able to understand how and why exposure works the way it works.

Camera set to
-3.0 Exposure

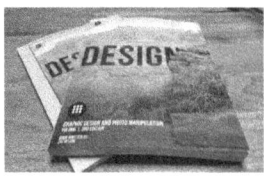

Camera set to
Auto Settings

Camera set to
3.0 Exposure

Couple of things. First, we can see that exposure matters. Second, we can see that the automatic settings are probably the best thing to leave the camera on. Yet, you still need to know how exposure works. As I stated earlier, its a fundamental of photography, its how your shot is lit. Lastly, we can tell the Exposure Scale. Exposure ranges from -3 to 3. The lower the number, the darker the image will come out.

ISO refers to the measure of sensitivity of the image sensor. A higher ISO means that your camera will become more sensitive to light, which would be better in a darker situation. Here's an example, 2 images with differing ISOs in differing environments:

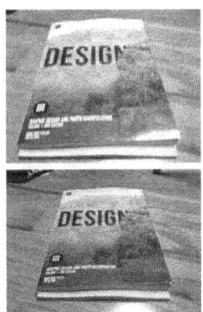
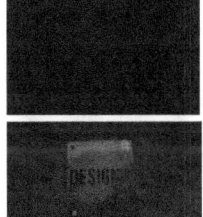

Camera set to **25 ISO**

Camera set to **2000 ISO**

You'll start to notice my statement from earlier. The photo with the higher ISO setting means that we can barely, yet still, see the book on the ground. A higher ISO will yield better results in a dark environment. Consider the factors, such as an action shot, before adjusting the ISO. Adjusting the ISO to make it higher will make your photo more grainy, so that's something else to consider.

THE FRAME OF THE CAMERA

Let's take a look at the body of a basic DSLR camera. Note that bodies will differ in structure and placement of buttons, so be sure to view your camera's manual to see detailed diagrams on where everything is.

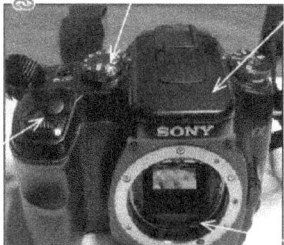

Presets Wheel: Allows the swapping of camera presets.

Flash: Pops out when you need a flash for low light situations.

Shutter Button: Takes the photo, and activates the Auto Focus.

Lens Mount: Allows the mounting of an external lens.

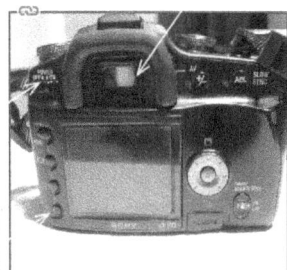

Viewfinder: Allows you to see what your taking a photo of.

Power Switch: Turns the camera On and off.

Playback Button: View Images and photos you've taken.

I labeled most of the features commonly found on a camera. Since my camera is a little older, some newer buttons may exist on the camera. Like I said earlier, be sure to check your camera's manual to see a detailed diagram and functionality of your specific model.

Now that we know and understand the basics of the DSLR camera, we can begin to discuss Lenses. In the next section, we will continue elaborating on some of the terms we discussed in this chapter and apply what they mean in the lens.

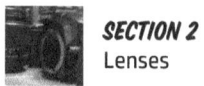

SECTION 2
Lenses

Lenses are the life stone of the camera. Obviously, without one, your camera would be a bare bones body. Yet, as we will begin to discover, lenses come in all different shapes and sizes. With that, this will require you to pick and choose the correct lens to fit the job.

As we discussed earlier, a **lens** is a finely ground and polished piece of glass that is coupled with a shutter to attach to a camera. They can be mounted in a cylinder that can move the lens back and forth to allow focusing the image on the sensor or film plane.

Simple lenses may be a single piece of glass like you see in a magnifying glass. They could have a convex or concave shape depending on the application and purpose intended for the lens. More complex lenses will be made up of multiple pieces of glass.

Lenses are primarily identified by their focal lengths such as 35mm, 50mm, or 125mm for example. The focal length means distance from the lens to the plane that will capture the image. The shorter the focal length the wider area you can capture on the image sensor of film. The longer the focal length the less area will be captured on the sensor or film. Also available are zoom lenses that allow you to vary the focal length. A 35-80mm zoom lens means that you can manipulate the focal length of the lens from 35mm up to 80 mm and any of the focal lengths in between those numbers.

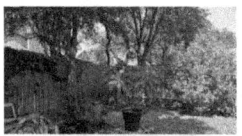
Fixed focal length of 28mm (also known as wide angle lens). Wide angle lenses are good for landscape photography.

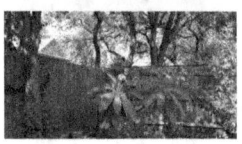
Fixed focal length of 50mm (fairly common fixed lens also know as "nifty-fifty"). Fixed focal length lenses from 50mm to 70mm are good for portrait work and generally any kind of photography.

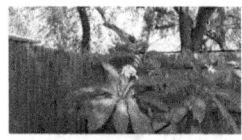
Variable focal length, 55-300mm Zoom Lens, at 55mm focal length.

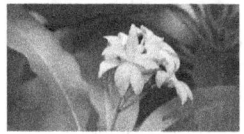
Variable focal length, 55-300mm Zoom Lens, at 300mm focal length. Zoom lenses provide flexibility for capturing wild life or other images where you may be limited in your access for a closer look or composition.

For example a 35-80mm zoom lens means that you can manipulate the focal length of the lens from 35mm up to 80 mm and any of the focal lengths in between those numbers.

When it comes to using Lenses across camera brands, the answer is confusing, as each camera manufacturer has its own specific connecting interfaces between camera body and any electronic controls for the lens that the camera will communicate. Examples are any of the automatic features the lens may contain like auto focus, and of the automatic program features the lens may contain. Yet, a provisional answer to the question is yes but an additional adapter that may be available that will allow you to use one lens brand on a different brand camera. Any automatic features of the lens may or may not be available, however.

The parts of a lens include the glass elements, and a shutter. The shutter has an aperture that can be opened to allow light to enter the camera that can also be held open for a period of time. The size of the shutter opening will also help you determine the lens you want to have for your camera.

Now that we have a basic understanding of Lenses, we can begin to develop our knowledge of the Camera and begin to take some photos.

SECTION 3
Additional Equipment

The best part about DSLR cameras is that they can be customized to the brim. There are plenty of accessories to add to improve your experience, as well as make your camera better. I want to discuss a few common accessories that you can use with your camera.

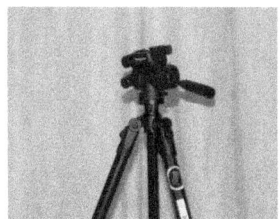

TRIPOD
Coming from the Greek prefix of TRI, a Tripod has 3 legs, standing your camera up so no one has to hold it. This allows users to take photos without having to be at the realm of controlling the camera. It also allows for stable shots and easy framing.

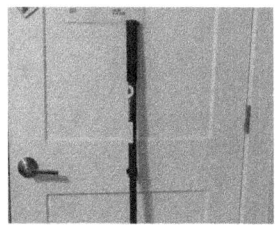

MONOPOD
Coming from the Greek prefix of MONO, the Mono pod allows for easy holding and on-the-go transport of the camera. Instead of setting up a clunky tripod, this one legged stick allows you to get a stable shot of landscapes. It is also known as the Photographers Walking Stick.

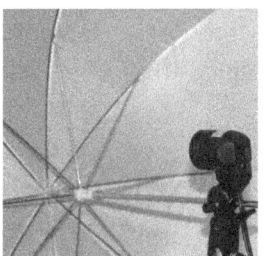

UMBRELLA LIGHT
The Umbrella Light helps balance the lighting by emitting a soft white light onto the subject, making the lighting balanced and look better on the final image.

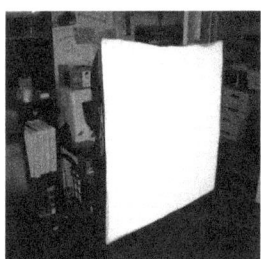

DIFFUSER LIGHT
Like the Umbrella light, this helps by diffusing light onto the subject, balancing and emitting light onto just the subject through a window-like white screen.

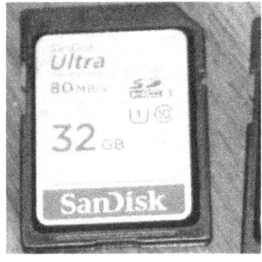

SD CARD
These little buddies are the lifeblood of your camera. They allow your photos to be stored and saved for sharing and editing. Without it, you won't be able to take photos, so be sure to not lose it!

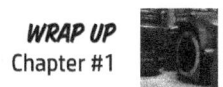

WRAP UP
Chapter #1

A WORD FROM ZAC

Although it may seem like a tsunami of vocabulary, understanding these terms will lead to your amazing success in Photography. Yet, it's important to know one thing: All cameras differ. Some cameras will require you to focus, while others will not. As Grandpa Larry discussed in Chapter #2, some lenses have features built into them that require the branded lens. For instance, a Sony lens may require a Sony camera. These connections and realizations are important to understand and comprehend, as you don't want to be throwing your money at a wall.

VOCABULARY FROM THIS CHAPTER:

- DSLR Camera
- Camcorder
- Camera Phone
- Social Media
- Studio
- Point and Shoot
- Full Frame
- Body
- Lens
- ISO
- Simple Lens
- Tripod
- Mono pod
- Umbrella Light
- Diffuser Light
- SD Card

GOOD OL' GRANDPA ADVICE:

Learn how to use your equipment:
 - Read the manual.
 - Practice in different light conditions.
 - Experiment with the different settings.
 - Look for interesting things to capture.
 - Learn how to keep your equipment clean and in good working order.

Now that you are familiar with your equipment you can start thinking about some of the other aspects involved in photography. BUT don't forget these basics and practice, practice, practice!

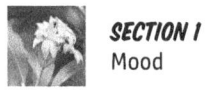

SECTION I
Mood

A lot of photographers don't understand the power and impact of tone and mood. While tone is important, mood refers to the viewer's impression. This means, when a viewer looks at a photo, they get an initial reaction. That reaction refers to their mood, whether it be happy, sad or nostalgic. I want to discuss some common moods and how to plan a mood for your photos.

First, there's the **subject**. The subject is the overarching premise for your mood. They're the focal point of the photo. Yet, you can manipulate the subject to affect the mood. Some obvious examples would be to manipulate the subject. For instance, if the subject was smiling, then the viewer may feel happy and cheerful. Yet, if the subject was frowning or crying, then the viewer may feel said. These are some ways to achieve mood in Subject Photography. Nature and Sports photography are kind of hard to manipulate, as the subject is concrete or non-controllable. Yet, you can still influence the photos in other ways.

Framing is another element of achieving good mood. In the next section, I'll discuss how to properly achieve framing, but the way you frame your subject depends on the mood you're trying to achieve. Say you take a long shot of the city using a wide angle lens. You would probably think differently of these photos. Let's take Grandpa Larry's example of the flowers and apply mood to it

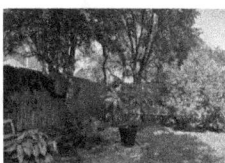 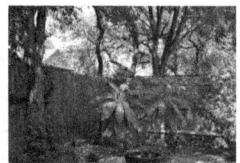 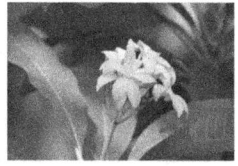

While these are all the same subject, they have different meanings and moods. Take the photo on the far right. The focal point is the flower. Yet, the focal point on the far left is still the flower "technically," as it has a longer shot of the entire garden. It gives viewers a broader picture of the setting and where the flower is compared to the flower itself.

Finally, and its probably the biggest, is **Lighting**.

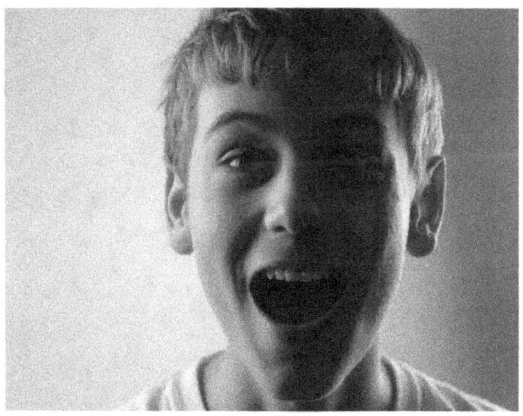

Ah yes, its 8th grade me. As we learned in this assignment in Middle School Newsmedia, lighting is key to capturing mood and impressions. Take this cringe worthy photo for instance. Notice my expression, its kind of happy, yet the lighting is dark and somewhat gloomy.

This is a perfect example of Lighting. Plenty of photos use lighting to capture and influence the viewer's mood about the photo. Blank and White may make a dramatic statement, while shadows create a ominous and dramatic effect. As we will discuss in the upcoming section, lighting is key to making your photography work for you.

In time, you'll learn how to influence mood in your photos. You can't concretely think and say what your viewers will think, but you can influence what they may think with these 3 areas.

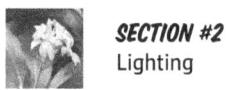

SECTION #2
Lighting

Lighting is one of the key factors in establishing mood. I made that clear in the previous section. There are some common ways to position your lights and subjects developed by industry professionals that I think it's worth a chat. These methods, of course, are recommended, and not required. But, they've been tested and used with Industry professionals, so I definitely think its worth a try to use and execute. Just know that these methods are designed for Subject Photography.

SPLIT LIGHTING

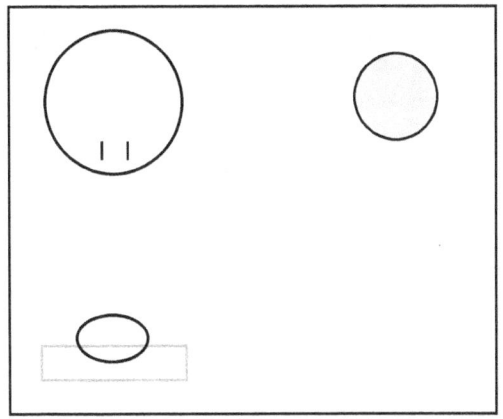

Light

A modified version of Split Lighting is one of the most commonly used methods. This method involves one subject, one light or natural light and one camera. All the objects form a Right, 90 degree angle at the subject, allowing for a dramatic effect or shadow on the subject.

LOOP LIGHTING

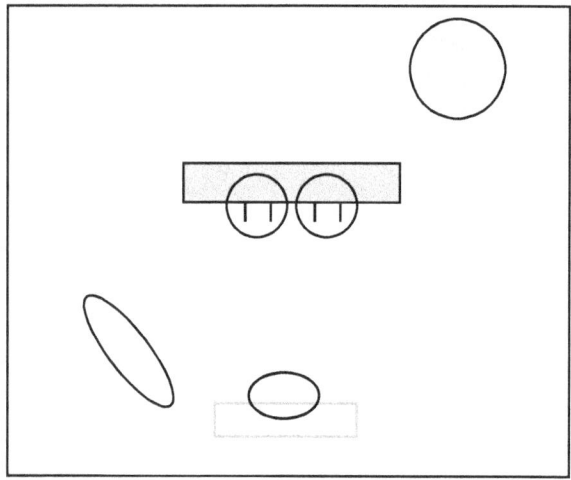

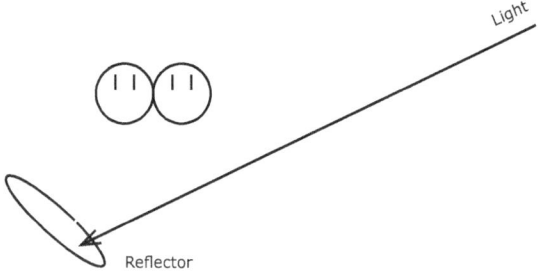

Loop Lighting is great for outdoor shoots. In this diagram, 2 subjects are presented against a backdrop, with a reflector reflecting Natural Light thats coming from behind. Loop Lighting allows for a somewhat evenly placed light with limited conditions and room for Artificial light.

REMBRANDT LIGHTING

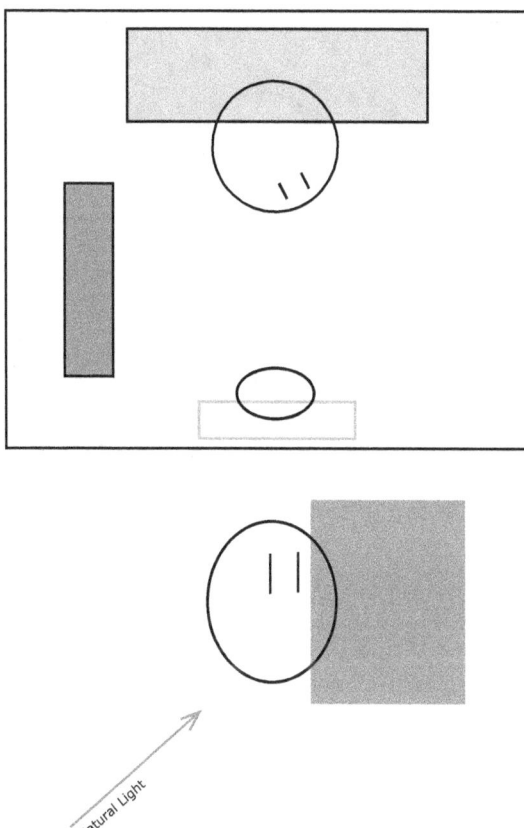

Rembrandt Lighting allows for limited resources, focusing on the element of Natural Light. In this example, the blue Box represents a Window. You want to position your camera and subject so that the Window or source of Natural Light can be sandwiched by the Subject and Camera.

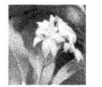 **BUTTERFLY LIGHTING**

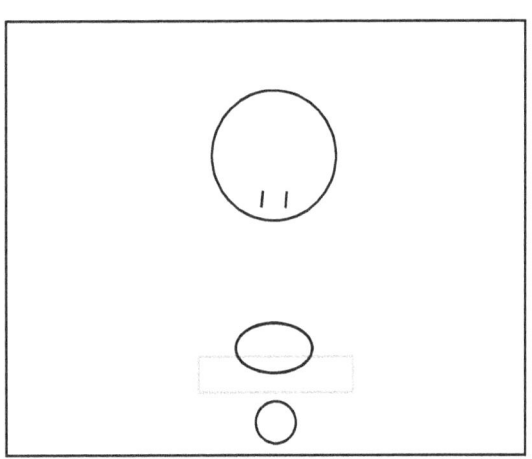

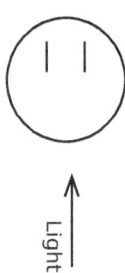

Butterfly Lighting is the most simplistic. It involves a straight line of sight. The light source is positioned at eye level with the subject and placed behind the camera, allowing for evenly lit situations.

BROAD LIGHTING

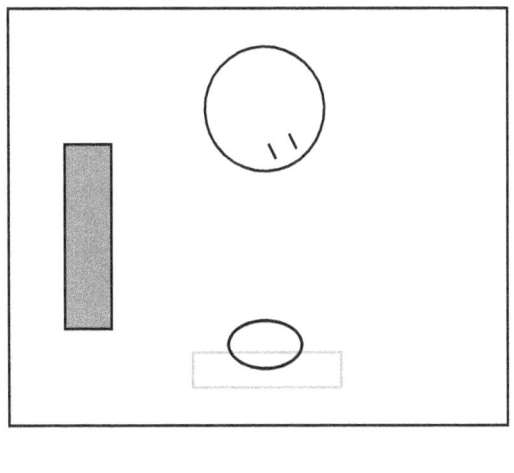

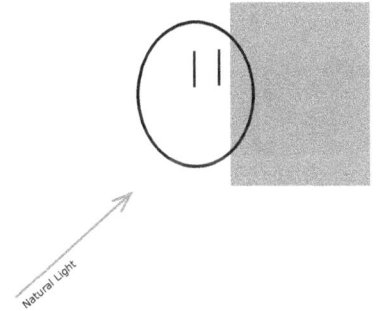

Broad Lighting is just like Rembrandt Lighting, EX-CEPT there is no concrete background. This means that the light won't be bounced or absorbed by the background, allowing for flexibility with the shot.

SHORT LIGHTING

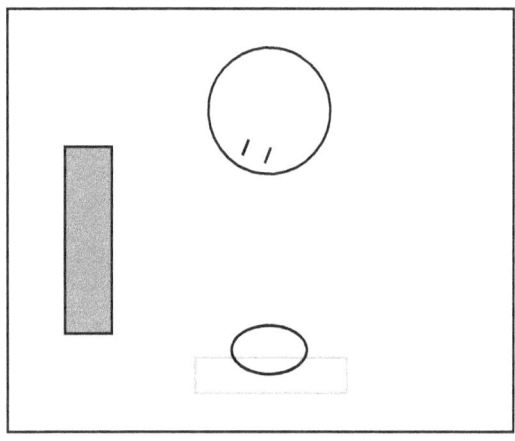

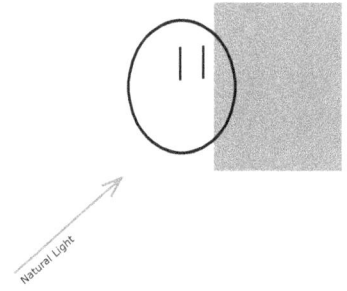

Short Lighting may look like Loop Lighting, but notice the Angle of the subject. The subject is facing the source of Natural Light, meaning the lit side of the face is now on the left side of the face rather than the right, which would be Loop Lighting.

LIGHTING DO AND DON'TS

Lighting is a KEY element in any photo. Let's discuss some DO's and DONT'S for working with Lighting.

DO USE NATURAL LIGHT WHEN YOU CAN
Natural Light refers to any sunlight coming through a Window. Natural Light makes any photo look more realistic than Artificial Light does, so if you have natural light, USE IT! However, you need a BALANCE of natural light so you don't have shadows, so be careful when using Natural Light!

DO ADJUST YOUR SETTINGS
It's important to adjust your Camera Settings, such as White Balance and ISO BEFORE you start shooting. For instance, a Gym or School has TERRIBLE lighting, so play around with your settings before you take a photo in order to ensure the maximum quality and exposure.

DO USE ARTIFICIAL LIGHTS WHEN YOU CAN
If you're in a room with no windows, you NEED to use Artificial lights! The tone of normal, overhead lights generally appear yellow and are not balanced. By following one of the methods presented in this chapter, you'll be able to evenly and properly light your photo and subject.

DON'T LET THE SETTINGS AUTO ADJUST
If you're in a setting with BAD LIGHTING, ALWAYS ADJUST YOUR SETTINGS MANUALLY! This is a good rule to follow, as the Automatic settings generally make your image more white than the natural yellow. Instead, adjust your settings to find a BALANCE between white and yellow.

DON'T WASH YOUR PHOTO OUT!
A **Washout** refers to your photo being overexposed and appearing too white. This makes your photo look weirdly white on the subject rather than balanced. Be sure to adjust the position of your artificial lights and how bright they are so you can avoid your subject being washed out.

AVOID GRAIN AT ALL COSTS!
Grain occurs when the settings of your camera aren't balanced or are adjusting weirdly, causing your photo to have "fuzz". This makes the photo appear like it's older and less clear. Instead, adjust your settings and turn off automatic functions when you're in badly lit areas, like gyms.

DON'T USE OVERHEAD LIGHTING!
Using too much overhead lighting can cause a unbalance of lighting in your image. Plus, in this example, a Washout of natural light occurs because of the far off window. It's important to understand the setting and what is around you when taking a photo, so be sure to remain aware!

SECTION 3
Positioning your Subject

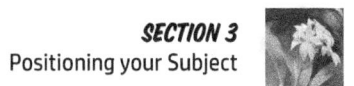

Let's discuss some rules of Photography that will help us not only establish a good shot, but also are some general practices that if followed, will result in some great looking photos.

THE RULE OF 3RDS
This is the biggest and most common rule in Photography. The Rule of 3rds is a rule for positioning your subject in a quadrant of 3 by 3 diagram. The idea for the rule is to not frame the subject in the center, but to compose the image with the main subject of interest positioned on one of the grids or at one of the intersections of the grids.

Here's an example:

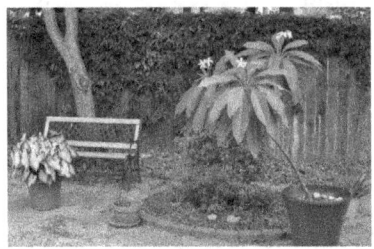

In this example, the photo has the main greenery with the three branches of blooms on the plumaria pretty well centered on the intersection of the upper and right grid lines.

Let's look at the photo with a Grid.

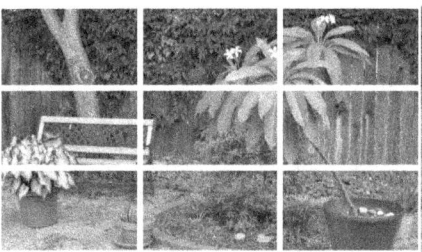

Now see how the plant is positioned?

Let's apply this to other types of photography, say Sports Photography. Now, I know what you're thinking, *"Zaaaac, this can't work because the subject is moving, not standing still!"* Oh, but yes it can work, through the power of editing. You see, later in the book, I'll discuss basic importing and editing of photos, and we will discuss how to crop photos, to which you can "cheat" and apply the Rule of 3rds, even if you didn't follow the rule the first time. Let's take another look at the rule in action in Sports Photography.

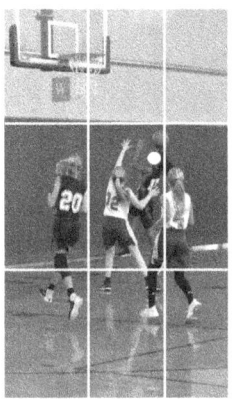

Rather than the subjects or people playing being the focal point, the basketball is the focal point, as it is at the center of the intersecting lines.

Let's look at some ways to position your subject.

In this example, the Yellow area represents **Empty Space**, something that "deters" the subject of the photo. By having Empty Space, you distract the viewer from the subject. As well, you're working your eyes to find the subject, instead of looking in the center.

In this example, the Yellow area represents **Headroom.** You want to have a minimal amount of headroom, but you still want to have headroom. If you have no headroom, then your subject's head will start to get cut off, making the photo look bad and wondering if the subject has a forehead at all.

LEADING LINES
Leading Lines is another great strategy to use. This strategy is more aimed for Nature photography rather than Subject Photography. **Leading Lines** refers to the composition where the viewer of your photo gets a sense of infinity. Let me show you an example.

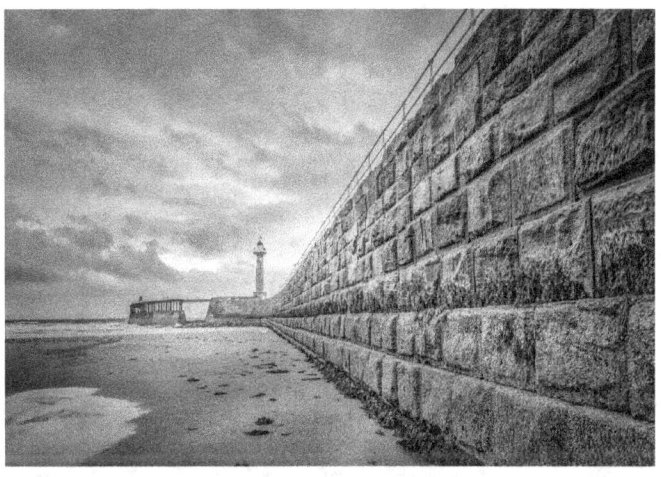

As you can see, you kind of get a sense that the wall goes on forever because the way the photographer angled the camera, the lens they chose and the overall composition. This strategy, yet, breaks the rule of 3rds, but for good reason. Instead of straining the eye, your eye directly jumps to the sensation of the wall, then your eye may start to follow the wall to see where it goes. This sensation can help your photos tell a story or give the viewer a sense of Illusion.

DIAGONALS

Diagonals are another great strategy to follow in Nature and Landscape photography. **Diagonals** refers to creating lines to draw a viewer through a photograph rather than tell a specific story. Here's an example:

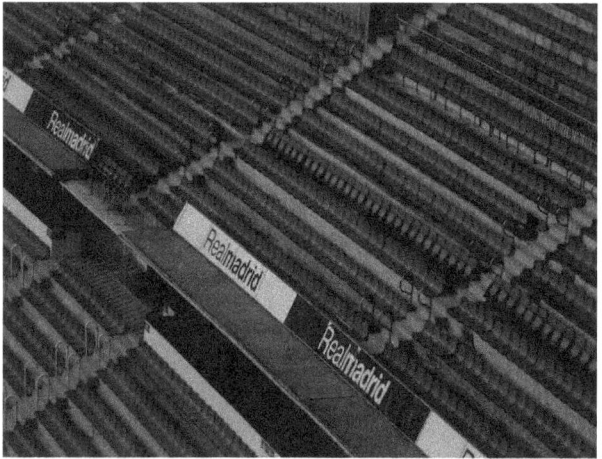

The items in this photo create some diagonal lines, creating some illusion and drawling your eye to the lines. While this is not the best example, it does demonstrate the concept well. I encourage you to look up Diagonal photos on the internet, as some are really clever and unique.

CONSIDER THIS
As we've discussed, there are 3 main strategies or illusions to keep in mind when positioning your subject and adding depth to your photo. But, I want to bring up a few points when taking photos that may seem like common sense, yet I see people break this all the time.

1. Consider your Location.
If you're taking photos of someone that's not on a neutral background, then that background better show some depth. For instance, say you're taking a photo of a student for a Yearbook quote. First, make sure you have a neutral background, like a white or black background with no posters or flyer's on the wall. If that's not possible, adjust the focus and see if you can take it in the hallway and blur the background. Rather than having just a beige locker, you have a background that is blurred showing depth and a focused subject. As well, be sure to not throw all the framing tips we've learned out the window. Center your subject, with minimal headroom and empty space.

2. Consider your Circumstance.
Think about the photo you're taking. Will it have multiple subjects, and if so, do you need a wider lens?

3. Consider the Situation
Finally, its important to consider your situation. You need to be aware of what you're taking a photo of, where you're taking the photo, and the reason you're taking that photo. Be prepared and have anything you need ready.

CAMERA ANGLES
Camera Angles refer to the distance between your subject and the camera. Let's discuss a few camera angles to use.

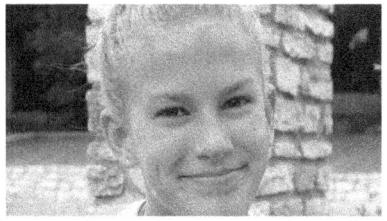

A **close up** is showing the subject, but the focus on one part of the subject. This may be the face, or a profile of the subject.

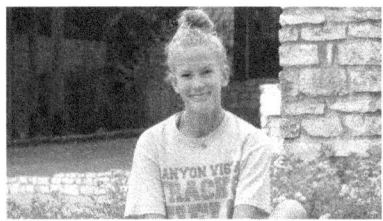

A **medium shot** may show the subject in view, but not completely in view. This may be from the torso up, or the torso down. This will show an equal amount of details and the subject.

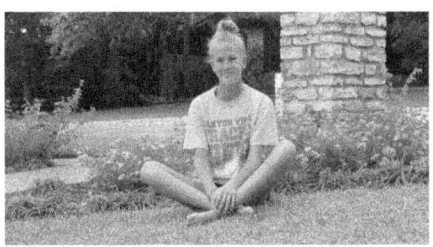

A **long shot** shows the subject in its entirety. This means, the subject is in view from head to toe. The details may be in view, but that is not the focal point of the shot.

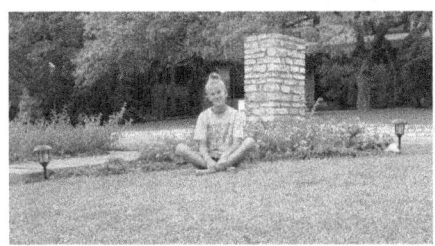

An **extreme long shot** shows the subject barely in view. The focus is mainly the setting or scenery, and the elements that fill it.

Note that these shots will still require you to use the Rule of 3rds, it applies to ANY shot at ANY angle!

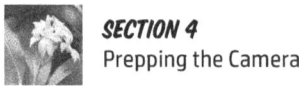

SECTION 4
Prepping the Camera

Now that we've learned all the basics and options provided by the camera, how do we apply this to initial situations? In this section, we will cover some missed ground that was presented in this section, plus discuss some ways to set up your camera in situations.

Focus refers to your subject being clear. You can manipulate the focus to make unique and interesting photos. Yet, focus can lead to your downfall, especially in Sports Photography, where the subjects are moving at a higher rate of speed than you are. It's important to be aware, as I've stated multiple times, of your situation and come well prepared.

Here are some examples of good use of focus and not so good:

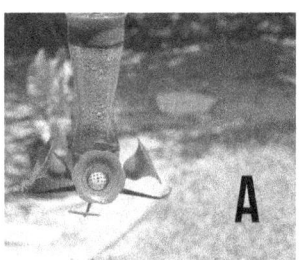
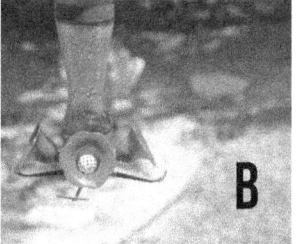

Let's try zooming in on the bird-feeder to see the difference up close:

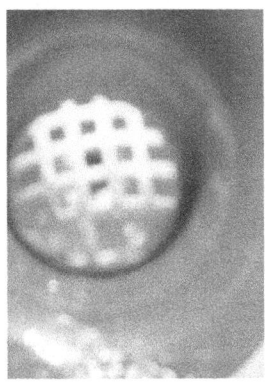

In this example, the focus is somewhat blurry. If you focus in on the flower/ending part of the bird-feeder, you may see that it is blurry.

The image shows the flower with the focus being less than sharp.

Although it may not appear blurry, put next to Example A, it does appear blurry.

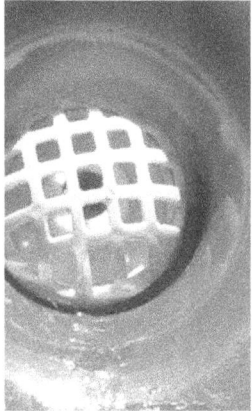

In this example, the background is blurred and the feeder, or the subject is in focus, it is as well clear.

This Image represents sharp focus on the flower on the feeder

Before venturing out for a photo shoot, and you have gone through your check list for all the items you will need with you, and they are all packed in your bag. Now you need to think about the conditions you will encounter during the shoot and what settings you should preset on your camera. The following things should be considered if your camera has all the capabilities of most modern DSLR cameras. In **manual mode** these are the settings that you can set:

White balance.

ISO.

Aperture.

Shutter speed.

Of course they can be changed if different conditions are encountered as your shoot progresses.

White balance is affected by the type of light that will be available and you should preset the camera for the lighting anticipated. For example bright sunlight, cloudy, full shade, incandescent, or fluorescent. Custom settings are also available. Review your owner's manual, and be aware of these alternatives also.

ISO is a setting for the light sensitivity of the camera's sensor. The brighter the light you expect the lower the ISO number should be set.

Aperture setting will depend on your subject whether stationary, or moving. The lower the number the larger the opening of the lens's aperture to allow more light into the exposure. The lower the smaller the opening. A sweet spot for a lot of lenses is an aperture setting of f/8.

The shutter speed is also dependent on your subject whether stationary, or moving. Moving subjects will require a faster shutter speed to stop the action without a blur.

CAMERA PRESETS

Most, if all, cameras have **preset** modes that you can toggle between to help the camera adjust in different situations. Generally, these are the same across cameras. Look for the Dial Wheel (I call it the Preset Dial) and see the icons. Some cameras have more icons, others have less icons.

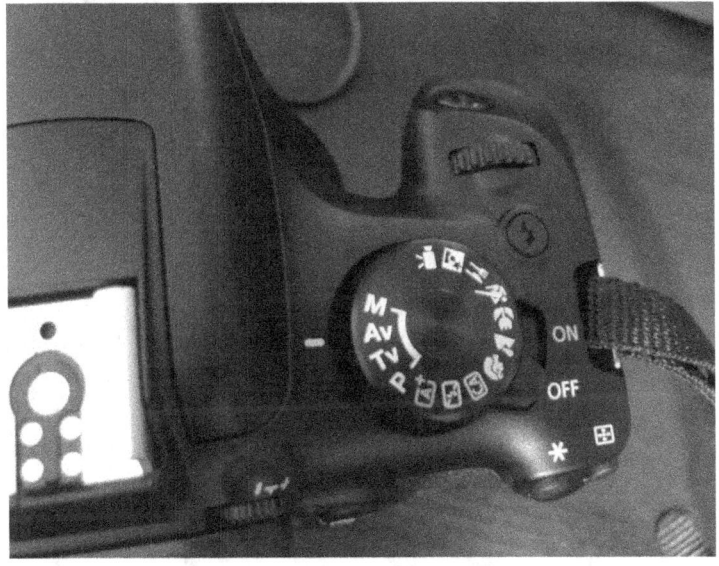

Presets are great, as they configure all the hard stuff for you. However, there are certain situations, such as flash, that will require the manual mode. Be sure to read your camera's provided manual to see what each preset does and means.

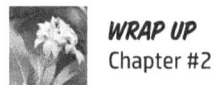
WRAP UP
Chapter #2

A WORD FROM ZAC

Now that we understand how to prepare the actual camera settings, we can begin to connect the vocab to the camera and certain situations. We learned how to frame our subject using the Rule of 3rds and some neat photography tricks, plus some lighting strategies and key elements, like Focus and White Balance. It may seem like another overload of vocabulary, but in time and with a little practice, your camera will become your soul-mate.

VOCABULARY FROM THIS CHAPTER:
- Subject
- Framing
- Lighting
- Split Lighting
- Loop Lighting
- Rembrandt Lighting
- Butterfly Lighting
- Broad Lighting
- Washout
- Grain
- Rule of 3rds
- Empty Space
- Head Room
- Close Up
- Medium Shot
- Long Shot
- Extreme Long Shot
- Focus
- White Balance
- Preset

This book is the work of my summer 2018. I started to pick up a passion for photography after my 7th grade year. While it was on the side burner of my bigger passion for Videography, I still had that spark and seed in me.

A few thanks are in order. First, thanks to my good ol' Grandpa Larry for helping me out in the areas I have truly not mastered yet. He helped contribute in some of the Lens and Framing your Subject sections. As well, he helped me take a lot of photos, since I did not have a DSLR camera at the time. (I was stuck with a 4K camcorder for the first half of this book). Plus, thanks to his wife, AKA Grandma Dee, TDW's exclusive editor and proofreader. Without her, this book would be nominated for Most Typos in an Educational Writing piece.

Also, thanks to my friends, Melinda and Rustin, for contributing some photos. Melinda's photos were featured a lot in Chapter 2's section headers. Rustin's photos were featured in some examples of what to do and not to do. Plus, thanks to my sister Claire for being my main model in some subject photos scattered throughout the book!

Finally, a big thanks to my middle school newsmedia teacher, Mrs. W! She actually planted the seed inside me to become the person I am today, not just in Photography, but in Videography and Design. Without her, I don't know if I would be writing these books today.

And thanks to all my readers! If you made it this far, you truly had some determination. On a final note, keep creating and taking great photos! Remember that you only get better if you try!

Until next time,
Zac DeLane

YOU'RE DONE!

Want to keep learning?
Try our Design Book about Graphic Design!

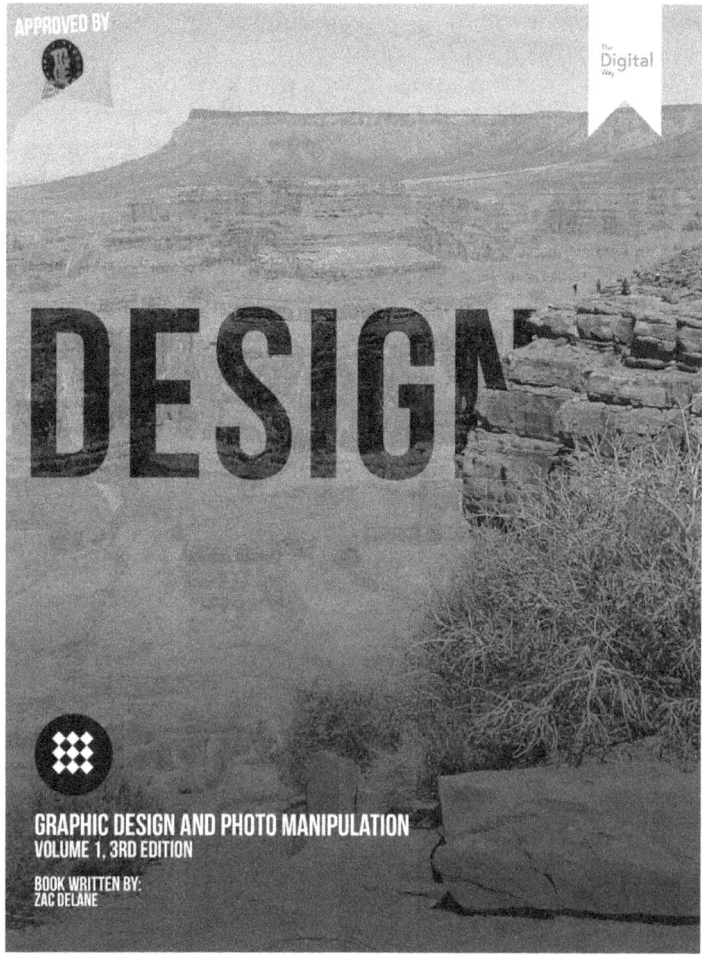

www.ingramcontent.com/pod-product-compliance
Lightning Source LLC
Chambersburg PA
CBHW030037230526
45472CB00002B/552